The Little Brown
HERO DOG

JAMES JERNIGAN

Fulton Books, Inc.
Meadville, PA

Published by Fulton Books 2019

ISBN 978-1-63338-910-6 (paperback)
ISBN 978-1-63338-911-3 (digital)

Printed in the United States of America

DEDICATION

This book is dedicated to all loyal pets, service animals and all the men and women serving or who have served in our military.

CONTENTS

CHAPTER 1

Who, How, and When

My name is James "Hank" Jennings. I was born December 15, 1947, in Birmingham, Alabama. I grew up in a small town outside of Birmingham known as Tarrant City, Alabama. I had an older brother and sister who I loved very much, but like all families growing up in the so-called happy days, we fussed a lot. I loved my mom who had a way of controlling us, whether it was falling on the floor, faking a heart attack, or threatening to tell our dad we would stop. We did not want the belt in the wood shed.

I remember one time, my brother and I got into a wrestling match, and he threw me into the mantle, and it broke our mom's favorite candy dish. We weren't poor but far from rich, and my mom loved that dish. Being resourceful, we glued it back together with airplane glue. Years later, our mom told us she knew because we had glued the red bird handle on backwards. *What a mom.*

My sister and I had the same type of relationship. She and her friend would hold me and put me in a baby carriage and push me in the neighborhood, but I knew one day I would get bigger, and that day came. She was climbing up on the porch by a rope I was holding about ten feet high, and about that time, I had a flashback about that baby carriage. *Boom*, I let go of the rope. My revenge was complete. She was bruised and had a bloody nose—so sorry. Boy was I sorry when Dad got home, and we headed to the woodshed. He told me the best form of revenge is *forgiveness* between licks with the strap.

My dad was a big man who had played baseball in the Memphis Chick organization and worked for the railroad. As I look back now, men and women who came through the depression and the two world wars became a different breed of people. They loved their country, their fellow man, no matter what color, and they loved God. I feel like my hard work, generosity, and love of God and country came from that background.

4

As the years passed, the *happy day* era began to come to a close. The Vietnam War was lingering on the horizon, and the US became more involved every day. My first real thoughts of the war came at the local swimming pool the summer of 1964. One afternoon, a friend of ours was called out of the pool, and we could hear her crying. We all ran to her, and she said she had to get home. Her family had been notified that her brother had been killed in Vietnam. Now each day, we began to think about our future. Graduation was in 1966, and now the draft was in place. This means you have to go and serve your country.

We began to think about what college or our future was going to be. I had already accepted a scholarship to play baseball at a junior college. One of my best friends was killed in 1967 and another in 1968, and I knew what I had to do—Vietnam here I come. I enlisted in the Army and was assigned to the air cavalry. We arrived in Saigon to blistering heat with bugs bigger than your fingers, and it never stopped raining.

CHAPTER 2

The Mischievous

I was sent to a base camp called Monkey Mountain. I was lucky to have an experienced commanding officer and gunnery sergeant who kept us as safe as they could. We were a mixture of soldiers from Alabama, Florida, New York, Maine, etc. One of my favorites was a soldier we nicknamed the jokester because he was always pulling pranks on all of us. We had been on patrol one night, and we were all tired, as I climbed into my sleeping hammock, something began to move. I began to scream at the jokester, "Not to night, I want to sleep."

As I begin to investigate, it was a plump ball of brown fur about the size of a football. I reached to throw it out, and it begin to lick me, but I was too tired to do anything else, so I let it sleep with me. When I awoke the next morning, it was snuggled up beside me, and we shared our C rations together. I could tell this was no run of the mill dog. It was dark brown with a stubby tail and curly fur on its ears. It had big web paws with hair on his feet that looked like he had boots on. He weighed about thirty pounds and was about twenty-four inches high. One of the fellows in the unit from South Carolina said that this is a Boykin duck dog better known as a Little Brown Dog. We figured he was about eight months old, and he had come over with an officer, who is a person of importance. Somehow he had gotten lost and made his way to Monkey Mountain.

The jokester had met his match in the dog we named Beaudreaux. He wandered around the camp, always bringing home some good snacks. We showed him what candy looked like, and he raided the jokester and got all his candy and cookies he had received from home.

CHAPTER 3

The Battle

Beaudreaux was not just a scavenger but a soldier, he could sense trouble. We did not know, but the Viet Cong had a plan to overrun our base camp that night. Beaudreaux had been barking and going crazy all day. We knew something was wrong, and we had to get ready. We shored our fences and doubled the lookouts. We were ready and repelled their attack time, and again, thanks to Beaudreaux for the warning. As the battle raged, Beaudreaux would go from one place to another and bark to let us know they are trying to get through the wire.

Beaudreaux was wounded in his foot and would walk with a limp forever. The medics took care of him like the soldier he was. He was awarded the purple heart and a medal for valor and bravery by our CO. From that day on, Beaudreaux was with us on the patrols and became my best friend.

CHAPTER 4

The Savior

We were sent into an area outside of our base camp where enemy activity had been reported. We all had a bad feeling about this mission. As we moved out, Beaudreaux was in my Alice backpack with all the ammo and C rations. His head looking over my shoulder, scouting the horizon for danger. We spread out and settled into a night's sleep with Beaudreaux beside me. I was on watch, and about 4:00 a.m., Beaudreaux got nervous, and I knew something was going to happen. My rifle was locked and loaded. Beaudreaux and I began to wake the other men when we came under heavy enemy fire.

We begin to return fire, and we realized we had been surrounded and were outnumbered. As I saw my fellow soldiers go down one by one, Beaudreaux would crawl through the jungle, dodging bullets to get to the wounded soldier. He would howl to let us know their position so we could work our way to them and pull them back to safety. One after another, he crawled, and he howled never leaving the soldier until we could get to them and bring them back to safety. All in all, about nineteen men were pulled to safety due to Beaudreaux howling. Reinforcements arrived. As the men were airlifted to safety, they kept screaming where is our Beaudreaux! They did not want to go unless they knew that Beaudreaux was safe. He had become a *savior* in the jungle night to the wounded men.

CHAPTER 5

The Medals and Coming Home

My tour of duty was over, and the CO wrote a letter to his commanding officer to allow Beaudreaux to come back to states with me. My wife and I had been living a quiet life traveling from Destin to Smith Lake. He loved the water and would ride in the boat every day, but we knew he needed a pal. I found a kennel in North Alabama that raised Boykins, and he had one female, the runt of the litter left. It was road trip time for me, my wife, and Beaudreaux. Now Beaudreaux had his pal, a feisty little female, named Bella. About a year later, we got a letter and two plane tickets to Washington, DC. The president was awarding Beaudreaux with the highest medal of all— the MEDAL OF HONOR. Of the nineteen men he had saved, eleven were in attendance. It was something to see, the little brown dog limping into the oval office with his head held high, accompanied by Bella and the eleven men in full salute. They let me put the medal around his neck, and he gave one of his famous *howls* as we left the oval office. We can all rest easy, knowing Beaudreaux, Bella, and the newest addition, Annie, a German short-haired pointer were on the prowl.

Get ready for round two as Beaudreaux is called out of retirement.

CHAPTER 6

The Loyalty of Man's Best Friend

NEVER LET ANYBODY TELL YOU ANIMALS, WHO ARE GOD'S CREATURES HAVE NO SOUL—THEY CAN BE YOUR BEST FRIEND AND PAL, NEVER ASKING FOR ANYTHING BUT LOVE.

My wife of fifty years instilled in me the love for dogs. I have always loved animals. We have had rabbits, goats, ponies, cats, dogs, and they are all special. Today we have two Boykin's, Bella and Beaudreaux and one German short-haired pointer named Annie. There is never a dull moment around the house.

The End for Now

ABOUT THE AUTHOR

James Jernigan grew up in a small town to the south of Birmingham, Alabama, called Tarrant City. He was taught southern values, love for God, family, and country. He has been married for fifty years, and his wife gave him his love for animals.

CPSIA information can be obtained
at www.ICGtesting.com
Printed in the USA
LVHW020030090221
678790LV00008B/252